From Seed to Apple Tree

By STEVEN ANDERSON

Illustrated by MARCIN PIWOWARSKI

CANTATA
LEARNING

MANKATO, MINNESOTA

WWW.CANTATALEARNING.COM

CANTATA LEARNING

MANKATO, MINNESOTA

Published by Cantata Learning
1710 Roe Crest Drive
North Mankato, MN 56003
www.cantatalearning.com

Library of Congress Control Number: 2014957001
978-1-63290-264-1 (hardcover/CD)
978-1-63290-416-4 (paperback/CD)
978-1-63290-458-4 (paperback)

From Seed to Apple Tree by Steven Anderson
Illustrated by Marcin Piwowarski

Book design, Tim Palin Creative
Editorial direction, Flat Sole Studio
Executive musical production and direction, Elizabeth Draper
Music arranged and produced by Steven C Music

Printed in the United States of America.

VISIT
WWW.CANTATALEARNING.COM/ACCESS-OUR-MUSIC
TO SING ALONG TO THE SONG

Every plant changes as it grows. An apple tree starts as a tiny seed. A **sapling** sprouts from that seed, growing **roots** and branches. When the tree is **mature**, it will bear fruit. More apple trees can grow from the seeds in the fruit. This series of changes is called a **life cycle**.

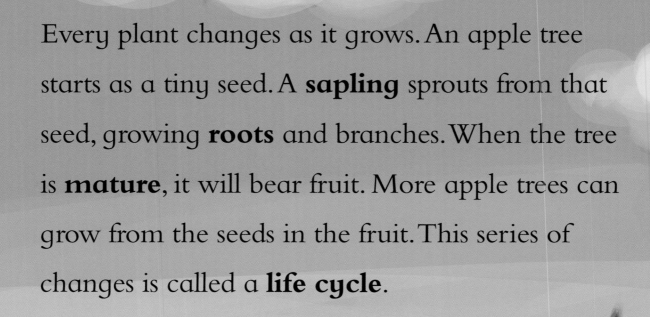

Now turn the page,

and sing along.

Sun, soil, and air are magical, you know.

Mix them with a seed, an apple tree will grow.

The seed sends out roots
to hold itself in place.

A sapling sprouts leaves
and catches the sun's rays.

There's a cycle of life
for all living things.

Apple trees begin as seeds
and then start growing
up, up, up so very tall.

The cycle's never ending.

Season after season, the apple tree **matures**.
Its buds bloom into pink-and-white flowers.

If a buzzing bee visits, bringing some **pollen**,
from each pretty flower an apple will ripen.

There's a cycle of life
for all living things.

Apple trees begin as seeds
and then start growing
up, up, up so very tall.

The cycle's never ending.

Apples are a tasty fruit
that people like to eat.

Buy them at the store
or pick them off a tree.

And inside each apple,

there are seeds, you know.

With sun, soil, and rain,

a new apple tree will grow.

There's a cycle of life
for all living things.

Apple trees begin as seeds
and then start growing
up, up, up so very tall.

The cycle's never ending.

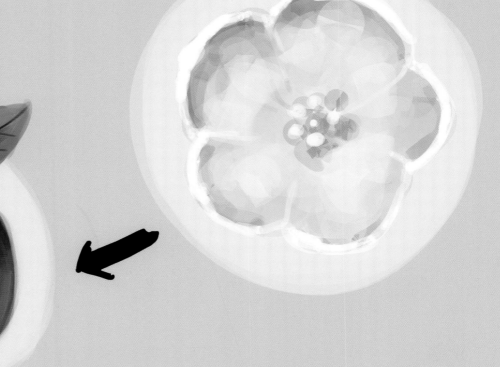

SONG LYRICS
From Seed to Apple Tree

Sun, soil, and air are magical, you know.
Mix them with a seed, an apple tree
   will grow.

The seed sends out roots
to hold itself in place.

A sapling sprouts leaves
and catches the sun's rays.

There's a cycle of life
for all living things.

Apple trees begin as seeds
and then start growing
up, up, up so very tall.

The cycle's never ending.

Season after season, the apple tree matures.
Its buds bloom into pink-and-white flowers.

If a buzzing bee visits, bringing some pollen,
from each pretty flower an apple will ripen.

There's a cycle of life
for all living things.

Apple trees begin as seeds
and then start growing
up, up, up so very tall.

The cycle's never ending.

Apples are a tasty fruit
that people like to eat.

Buy them at the store
or pick them off a tree.

And inside each apple,
there are seeds, you know.

With sun, soil, and rain,
a new apple tree will grow.

There's a cycle of life
for all living things.

Apple trees begin as seeds
and then start growing
up, up, up so very tall.

The cycle's never ending.

From Seed to Apple Tree

Verse 2
Season after season,
the apple tree matures.
Its buds bloom into
pink-and-white flowers
If a buzzing bee visits,
bringing some pollen,
from each pretty flower
an apple will ripen.

Chorus

Verse 3
Apples are tasty fruit
that people like to eat.
Buy them at the store
or pick them off a tree.
And inside each apple,
there are seeds, you know.
With sun, soil, and rain,
a new apple tree will grow.

Chorus (2x)

GLOSSARY

life cycle—a series of changes that a tree goes through, from seed to growing into a full-grown tree

mature—fully grown

matures—to grow

pollen—particles that trees need to bear fruit

roots—the parts of a tree that grow down into the ground; roots support the tree, and they also get water and nutrients from the ground.

sapling—a young tree

GUIDED READING ACTIVITIES

1. What things help a seed grow into an apple tree?

2. Do you like apples? Why or why not? What are the different ways you can eat apples?

3. What are the stages of an apple tree's life cycle? Can you draw them?

TO LEARN MORE

Faundez, Anne. *Apples Grow on the Trees*. Mankato, MN: QEB Pub., 2013.

Griswold, Cliff. *Let's Go Apple Picking!* New York: Gareth Stevens Publishing, 2015.

Knudsen, Shannon. *Seed, Sprout, Fruit: An Apple Tree Life Cycle*. Mankato, MN: Capstone Press, 2011.

Owen, Ruth. *Fruit!: Life on An Apple Farm*. New York: Windmill Books, 2012.